INTRODUCTION

Margaret N. Popov was born on June 27, 1945 in the Kentfield-part of Marin General Hospital[1] in San Anselmo, CA. She was born to Dr. Nicholas Paul Popov and Margaret Nicholas Popov.

At approximately the age of 2 to 3-years of age, Margaret's parents first noticed something "different" about their daughter. As a child, Margaret struggled with visual hallucinations, which frightened her all day and night. It was not until she was older that she was finally diagnosed with Schizoaffective Disorder.

Schizoaffective Disorder is a combination of symptoms of schizophrenia and mood disorder, such as depression or bipolar disorder. Symptoms may occur at the same time or at different times. Cycles of severe symptoms are often followed by periods of improvement. Symptoms may include delusions, hallucinations, depressed episodes, and manic periods of high energy.

By the time Margaret was in her fifties, she finally received the medication she needed to help her cope with her illness. Margaret says, "Modern medicine is a miracle and it saved my life." Thanks to her current and ongoing medication regimen, Margaret is able to live a happy, productive and prosperous life. In fact, it was her dream to become a professional musician and a published author.

As a professional musician, Margaret played piano for many private concerts. While she never performed with other musicians, she was quite content performing in more intimate settings. She did this for many years and continues to play the piano for herself at the board-and-care house she's currently living in.

Most recently, now that Margaret is in her 7th decade of life, she decided she wanted to become a published author. Her idea was to publish poems she had written over many years. Some of her poems talk about people that cared for her or other topics she simply wanted to write about. Other poems talk about the pain and her own personal experiences living with her illness. That is why she wanted to name this book, "Poems of a Crazy Woman." While some maybe put-off by the title, this was the title she came up with after she finished writing the final poem. "The name of my book seems appropriate," says Margaret.

In closing, Margaret is living on a fixed-income. She is hoping proceeds from this book will continue to provide her with the little extras she appreciates that helps improve her quality of life, like paying for Russian-language television on Direct-TV or going to Panda Express once a month. Therefore, if you purchased this book, Margaret would like to give you a heartfelt "thank you" and "God bless you."

- Compiled by Robert E. Garcia, RN

---

[1] Marin General Hospital is physically divided by two different cities (Kentfield and Greenbrae, CA)

TABLE OF CONTENTS

Onset of Schizoaffective Disorder

I died when I was fourteen;

life seemed so dark and cruel,

where left the kindness, it was mean;

a knife cut fit to cut a jewel.

The years behind seemed like a dream

and all that's good seemed left behind;

things are worse than what they seem

I became a prisoner of my mind.

And as the panorama of our life unfolds

a certain medication may give us some hope.

"the greatest story" ever told,

may help give us our ability to cope.

Nonetheless, it is still worth the fight

the universe is filled with beauty rare,

though from reality we take our flight,

we have a temporary cross to bear.

Each year we become somewhat less blind

though life's lessons may seem quite severe.

We need to learn a lesson of another kind,

we need to learn to feel God's presence very

near.

2

our days are numbered

so let's make the most;

we must have slumbered;

but let's make a toast;

we love old-fashioned funnies;

and friendly ghosts.

Greece and Rome

I would like to write a poem

concerning ancient Greece and Rome.

the Romans invented what we call roads

made for passengers traveling with loads.

Rome was the center of inherited culture

of Greek architecture and skillful sculpture.

Greeks were adept at speeches, oration;

their philosopher's spent time in much meditation.

the pantheon and Colosseum

are like a modern-day outdoor museum.

these two civilizations helped to pave the way

and to make the world what it is today.

PURGATORY ON EARTH

WE FEEL SO MANY JOYS,

DURING OUR PURGATORY HERE ON EARTH,

WE'RE GLAD TO BE ALIVE AGAIN,

AND THAT WE've been given birth.

Each of our lives is A JOURNEY,

WITH LESSONS TO BE LEARNED.

WE SUFFER; WE LIVE; WE LAUGH; WE CRY;

WE LEARN AND HAVE DISCERNED.

THE LOVE WE've shared while we are here,

with those we cherish and hold dear.

Or when we kneel down to thank the Lord,

for the victories we have won.

THEN OUR SIGHTS ARE SET;

WE DON't regret

our sad moods flee and they are gone.

Musical Building Blocks

A chord which acts as a type of gager

Is one which is common and simply called major.

One may debate if the sound is finer

produced by a chord which is called the minor.

A V7 sounding characteristically predominant

Is called with certainty the dominant.

Before the sevenths can be finished

We must include the half-diminished.

Though it's not something that is fixed

We sometimes have an added sixth.

The effect you will not halter,

By a chord that you will alter.

You don't need to play the flute

To build a chord upon the root.

Triads built upon the keys

Are bunched within a group of threes.

It Certainly was no added chore

To create sevenths in groups of four.

Besides the triads and the sevenths

There are the 9th's; 13th's; 11th's.

There are several different versions

That is why we have inversions.

Although the keys aren't made of boards

They're very good for building chords.

Whether you begin from the left or "middle C"

No matter what the clef

you create harmony.

Music consists of motives and phrases,

We love its cadences,

it inspires; amazes.

We need to ponder lots,

Over each and all of the musical thoughts.

Ludwig Von Beethoven Music: Part A

Beethoven has his name in the classical (musical) hall of fame.

When he could no longer hear a sound.

He composed music so unique and profound.

He took less of a chance

When it came to love and romance.

He was only content when he wrote

Note after note after note.

He would often conceive a tune

While he would walk through the woods and soon,

He would write it down right away

That was his only way.

We recall his famous quote

"I will seize fate by the throat"

"I will not let my infirmity (his deafness) get me down;"

Among musicians he wears a crown,

He will always be loved and renowned.

His name shall live on forever;

Mankind shan't forget him ever.

His art and his great endeavor;

Was sheer genius and not only clever.

His music seems so unreal

It is close to the very ideal;

It sets the wheels in motion

To feel deep and profound emotion;

It's just like some magical potion,

We owe him our love and devotion.

His nature was social and warm

His music created a storm.

He lived alone for his art

He uplifted the mind and the heart.

There often are many quarrels

Over who deserves the laurels,

But he will remain a rarity;

His name shall go down for posterity.

His music is widely developed

And many motives and themes have enveloped.

The sonatas make use of the various elements

Throughout recapitulations, expositions, and different developments.

His harmonies, forms and powerful pitch

Demonstrate sound so dynamic and rich.

Although in his day it wasn't the norm

He made order from chaos and created a form.

Civilization has already advanced

To give his music more of a chance.

His music is deep and very involved

A new style through Beethoven has surely evolved.

He was in advance of his time;

The classical style reached its climax and prime.

His form has real order as well as design.

Beethoven was the lonely rebel

He achieved a very high level.

He gives us an honest rendition,

Of our over-all human condition

(That was his goal and his mission.)

His music can set us afire,

And fill us with hope and desire.

The tones will tell us a story

Of despair, and then triumph and glory.

Beethoven's work was certainly worthwhile

He created a unique and original style.

He was the link between classical and romantic,

The over-all effect was overwhelming; gigantic.

He has beautiful design and delightful form,

We hear his willingness to conform.

Those who his music do understand

Will triumph o'er obstacles and more easily stand.

In his third period he composed with his inner ear,

He wiped away all doubt and all fear.

There was more shadow in his life than sunshine,

But his over-all spirit made a moving design;

He inspires us all with that which was sublime,

He is truly one of a kind.

His music sounds very orchestral,

We can compare it with the celestial.

Because he mastered his destiny and fate,

He will always be loved and considered great.

Ludwig Von Beethoven Music: Part B

Beethoven's music is delightful and charming,

it's dynamic in force, but by no means alarming.

it's rhythms; it's harmonies; its form and design

brings a sense of completeness which is almost divine.

when you hear a chord struck,

it gets one's attention,

what marvelous art, what a gorgeous invention!

His music evokes a sound that is great,

what can one say-but it's truly first-rate!

Playing Beethoven gives one joy,

it's a nice way for the time to employ.

His music gives us a sense of rapture,

each moment one wants to catch & to capture.

one gets a sense of sheer delight,

when the chords & notes, resound &take flight!

Pain

Oh, what agony I'm bearing.

Will our dear Lord see me through?

Will there be a new horizon?

Will there be some skies of blue?

When I feel such powerful heartache

is there anyone that cares?

Will fate give me some sweet solace?

Will I manage my affairs?

What will be around the corner

in this tortured, suffering life,

as we pause and lie and listen to the danger and the strife?

Someday they'll be sweet solace,

someday I'll find my peace;

in the meantime, we will struggle,

while our restless murmurings cease.

CHILDREN'S CLASSICS

ANNE OF GREEN GABLES

THE KNIGHTS OF THE ROUNDTABLES.

THE "LITTLE HOUSE" BOOKS

DO NOT DEAL WITH CROOKS.

"THE SECRET GARDEN" WILL SOFTEN; NOT

HARDEN, "SARAH'S IDEA" AND "HEIDI"

ARE WARM, CLEAR AND TIDY.

"UNDERSTOOD BETSY" AND "JANE EYRE"

GIVE US THOUGHTS SWEET AND FAIR.

"LITTLE WOMEN," "LITTLE MEN,"

CAN BE READ OVER AGAIN.

"ROBINSON CRUSOE" AND "TOM SAWYER"

ARE FULL OF ADVENTURES.

READING GOOD BOOKS IS A WORTHWHILE

VENTURE.

HOW THE INDIANS FOUGHT

AND THE PIONEERS TRAVELED WEST

WE HAVEN'T FORGOTTEN THEIR RIGOROUS

TEST.

"LITTLE RED RIDINGHOOD," "GOLDILOCKS"

BRER RABBIT AND RENARD THE FOX.

"THE THREE BEARS;" "THE TORTOISE AND

THE HARE."

INCLUDED IS THE DISCOVERY OF GOLD

AND THE TALES OF "THE MERRY HEARTS

AND BOLD,"

THESE ARE TALES THAT NEVER GROW OLD.

WE WATCH IN SUSPENSE

HOW THEIR PLOTS DO UNFOLD,

THEY CAN BE TOLD AND RE-TOLD AND RE-

TOLD.

Maria Alexandrovna

My dearest Maria Alexandrovna

You truly did amaze,

oh how I miss you dear one

I'm held in such a daze.

You took the place of mama,

you were the substitute;

of all OUR family drama,

then, I finally took a root,

your never-ending patience

bore lots and lots of fruit.

A Russian and Polish SWEET ONE

OH the sweet ones I have known

after I was supposed to be grown.

Or RHEA, sweet RHea (auntie) WHEN

we would go to the grocery store,

I used to admire you when we walked,

AND my heart was overwhelmed with love for yoU.

Rose would take us along

to you I did **belong,**

for a time considered long.

Now, I know A Maria WHOM I looked,

(AT THE CHRISTMAS PARTY THE OTHER DAY)

she was just so sweet and cute and lo*v*LY *in every sort of way.*

OH RHEA, *like a mama you*'ve taught me;

and you did it in the way which was excellently.

now, I am by myself AND CAN SURVive

This life, because, of Rhea

amidst all the dangerS, struggle and strife.

an older sister I inherited

for mAMA RHEA we *have merited,*

for you to be at peace

and for me to live on and release

(my feelings and thoughts through the pen).

Maria LLVOvNA

There is a real sweet lady whose name is Maria

she always comes up with many a bright idea

of interesting and lively thoughts

which I enjoy so lots and lots.

She was filled with fun and laughter,

which carried into the day here after.

She loves and enjoys music which is serious,

nothing to her seems too mysterious.

she is smart and cute and very much alive

she is certain to survive and to thrive.

she's very, very observant,

I love her and others with a love that IS FERVENT.

Suffering

The tears were shed; I felt pain

the tears were shed; but not in vain.

they cleared the air for a little joy

they didN'T spare us, or Annoy,

they provided gentle relief

they gave vent to sorrow and grief.

let's all hope next time we WeeP

will help us peacefully to sleep,

and HELP US SO OUR COURAGE KEEP.

PAIN WILL COME;

AND PAIN WILL GO.

WE FEEL HAPPIER,

OR, WE FEEL LOW.

EACH MOMENT ENDURED *is like a buffer,*

throughout the time that we may suffer.

Joyce and Jays Get-together

We had forgotten about our worries and Woes

and lo, and behold like we danced on our toes,

we wanted to forget The Mundane AND routine,

so we came to a home with a fairy book scene.

We can't leave out the beautiful combination

of the violin, the piano, and the following sENSATion;

IT gives us A feeling of elevation.

The CIDer was tasty and warm and delicious

(we certainly have eaten the very nutritious);

what a lovely, delightful and memorABLE daY

it will help us all, to feel OK!

Friendship

A friend in need is a friend indeed;
this is very real, you know just
how I feel.

She reached out to me,
when I was sinking.
In the sea of life,
This set me thinking.
Of adapting a change.
In my old life, to rearrange
that struggle and strife.

The old folks of Mirgorod (Russian)
is what she represents
the kindness, strictness, taking-care-of-ness,
to which I do consent.

Mrs. Poll

She has been a wonderful mother to Litvins (Anton and Mabel),

she's been a wonderful mother to me,

she's been A wonderful mother to Erika

open your eyes and see.

She has talked about our dear Jesus

she's been good; she's been smart; she was nice,

she taught me for life many practical things

she was full of **sugar and spice.**

She has taken good care of some people,

and plants and animals too,

she shared her home and was blessed,

and went through many a trial and test.

She was a beauty; she was kind.

I did the footwork; she was the mind,

she stood by me like a tigress;

and, I'll always love her dearly.

I was her creation.

she taught me how to give and take,

and to reciprocate.

she exposed me to our heritage,

she taught me how to survive,

she taught me how to cope,

to adjust and to thrive.

Drowning in Life

I was drowning, drowning, drowning

in the sea of life.

Only two or three could help me in this plight.

I felt myself sinking

I was unable to be thinking

save me, save me, save me from doom

isn't there some room?

Then like a salmon going upstream

to reach the top of the stream.

I fought like a hyena to join the team

of all the desperate people who are struggling so,

I don't know when this suffering will end

save me; save me; into the pit I descend

(but some wise soul gave me a Hand)

save me from destruction

wherever I stray,

and shine a light to point the way.

Outer space

When I look up at the stars

I often think of Mars.

in the month of June

I like to admire the moon.

The Milky Way has a lot to say

about God's creation and each constellation.

Of the planets we know

some in beauty a-glow.

don't forget the sun

it weighs many-a-ton

(yet none of it's craters

contain alligators).

The sun's distant rays,

give length to the days.

you need to look far

to see your way clear to a star.

Each country now has a base,

we are all caught up in a race,

we have all turned our face,

in our quest for outer space.

We study the earth's revolution,

and stay true to our constitution.

We study the earth's rotation,

and inspect the moon's gravitation.

and some teachers are hiring tutors

to teach their children computers.

This is the latest in style

we have traveled many-a-mile.

The Very Old

(Written when I was much younger)

I love the people who are very old

They seem to have a heart of gold

The very old are very wise,

Wisdom comes before one dies.

The very old need special care

This is only good and fair,

The old know lots about the life

Its struggles; it's turmoils; the trouble;

the strife.

It is important that you greet,

These people who are very sweet.

They seem so wise and truly smart

They touch you at the very heart.

The old are just a symbol of

An everlasting kind of love.

AUNTIE

WHO IS THIS ANGEL WHO ENTERED MY LIFE,

AMIDST ALL THE TURMOIL TROUBLE, AND STRIFE?

I WAS SO FRIGHTENED, SO TERRIBLY LOST,

SO UNENLIGHTENED, AT WHAT A COST,

WHAT IS THE RIDDLE OF LIFE,

FROM BEGINNING TO END?

WE NEED EACH OTHER, HOW WE NEED A FRIEND.

(I NEEDED YOU TO SURELY DEFEND.)

WHO IS THIS GOOD LADY WHO TOOK CARE OF ME?

WHO IS THIS SWEET LADY, WHO GAVE ME EYES TO SEE?

SOON SHE WILL REST IN TRANQUILITY.

SOON HER SOUL WILL BE SAFE AND FREE.

I'VE GOT TO TRY TO BE EXTRA GOOD.

I'VE GOT TO TRY TO DO THINGS I SHOULD.

I'VE GOT TO TRY TO BE A GIVER, NOT A TAKER.

SO I COULD LATER JOIN HER IN MEETING MY MAKER.

WE'LL LIVE ON HIGH WITH OUR DEITY,

WITH LOVE AND JOY THROUGH ETERNITY.

SHE WAS THE ONLY ONE WHO COULD HELP ME,

TO HER IT WAS SIMPLE AS A, B AND C.

NONE (I KNOW SO FAR) TO AUNTIE CAN COMPARE,

WHO CAN GIVE SUCH LOVING CARE.

Erika

There is a kindly lady named Erika ;

she makes her home in America ,

she never had a sister or brother

but, she made a wonderful wife and mother .

with her children she attunes to one wave length ;

this comes from maternal instinct and strength .

She likes the North Carolina scenery ,

her clothes she maintains like a regular cleaner .

she doesn't like to run or jog ,

but she loves her cat and her puppy dog .

it is essential to use a few words ,

to mention her liking of the Carolina birds .

She doesn't like to quarrel or fight

she would prefer to work, or to read or to write.

she has even mentioned and told,

how much pleasure she gets from her Own household.

She took care of mother when she was ill;

she gave her comfort, And water, and pills.

she even leaves her children and mate,

to visit mother in a different state (California).

For mother she has lots of love,

she is as gentle as a turtle dove.

Erika is easy, too -

down to earth and very true.

Men and women

Some men think they're better than women,

And I will tell you why

Men can live under the same roof together

They don't even have to try.

Women under the same roof together,

Are at each others throats.

It has nothing to do with the weather

It takes no famous quotes.

There's a comradery among the men,

Ironic but nonetheless exists.

There are various sorts of women

Men can sometimes be hard to resist.

Some men think they're better than women

Though there may be some doubt.

We need to build Up each other

Then, make our turn-about.

Life

People unfed feel pangs of hunger

Whether they're old, or whether they're younger.

People may experience cold,

Both the young and the very old.

There may be chronic unemployment,

This is usually no enjoyment.

There may be disillusion in romance,

But we can have another chance.

Work in life is our fulfillness

That's unless we have an illness.

Farms may lose what they have focused

When a crop is ruined by locusts.

When we join hands to help our fellow man,

we do the very best we can.

Floods, fires, hurricanes, tornadoes

all kinds of natural disasters

will make us think a little faster.

It is quiet before the storm

We may grieve, and we may Mourn.

Although money may be a chore

There's hardly worse than living through war.

If you've lost your general health,

Then there is no need for wealth.

When each family member makes their contribution

That's the very best solution.

There is pleasure; there is pain;

There is sunshine, after rain.

Thank You Mama for Our Pleasant Home

My "Mutti" (Mother in German) and I lived together

in our cozy, pleasant home.

there were hard times we would weather,

and solve them both alone.

We had a regular routine

for our necessary duties,

her sweetness I esteem

we lived in Burlingame and admired all its beauties.

sometimes we would have guests

she would cook; and I'd provide all the (musical)

entertainment,

and think of all the rest;

we needed no real payment.

She would send me off to church

to be among our people.

sometimes, they'd pick me up for services

to a beautifully decorated steeple.

She would dress me up and fix my hair

with her loving, artistic fingers.

she brought me up with love and care,

her memory forever lingers.

My heart she helped to re-soften

despite of family drama.

Sestron ("sister"), her daughter and I talk often

and we remember our dear mama.

Lovely People

Our auntie had integrity and was very wise

she very definitely has x-ray eyes,

she takes care of people and plants of all kind

she has a very practical frame of mind.

in her life she had to survive

She had to be able to live and to thrive.

she's been very understanding and knows how to forgive

she was strict and knows how to truly live.

she surely has the eyes of a hawk

but, she never especially liked to talk.

You could depend on her and trust her,

In her, you could confide;

she would not let you down, nor would she deride

she likes to sew and to cook;

she likes to read an intelligent book.

She loves to work in the great outdoors,

she insisted that I always do my chores.

she likes to study nutrition;

she used to be a beautician.

bright-eyed, energetic, and with bushytailed,

her love and attention have always prevailed.

in her youth if she happened to like whom she met,

she would then play the role of a little "coquette."

she hates to see birds locked up in the cage,

Unrighteousness makes her go into rage.

in Germany, she used to pick people off of the street

and find little ways how their needs she could meet.

she prayed to God that in her old age

not to go hungry and her prayers were heard,

by the time that she had into turned into a regular sage,

and found that the Lord had heard her words.

She certainly has not been a drone;

in her, there lieth no lazy bone

she enjoys the piano and the sound of its tone;

she likes to receive a call on the phone.

she worked hard all her life

and conquered all strife.

she loved me unconditionally; she did indeed

well in me she has certainly planted a seed.

good manners are to her as natural as can be,

she was a sweet lady and a beauty to see.

she loves to feed hungry men;

she has done it again and again.

she's always mended my socks;

she prided herself on being a fox.

she dressed me up; brushed me; and sent me to church.

she was the answer to part of my spiritual search.

I can say for a fact without negation

that I owe her my love and adoration.

by this time one can clearly see

that my dearest auntie means the world to me.

to me she is auntie, to you she is Nana

it can well be said, she's like heaven sent Manna.

A Troubled Conscience

I have such a sense of guilt,

I could just lie down and wilt.

I have such a sense of shame,

it causes me much pain.

Oh Lord, how you will judge me

is my earnest heartfelt plea?

To God I must account

my guilty feelings mount.

I face my guilt alone

to Him I must atone

(I stand before his throne.)

We have failed in many ways

he has numbered all our days.

I could tear myself apart;

I need a brand-new start.

I try to seek his face

will He save me his grace?

(And there are many others whom

a troubled conscience bothers.)

How can one escape

before it is too late?

We didn't ask for our own birth

we have had our hell on earth.

Does God love even me?

I wish I could clearly see.

Lord, will you us redeem?

Lord, will you intervene?

Ourselves we can't forgive;

with ourselves we cannot live.

The Tears Still Fall

The tears still fall

But, the torment is gone,

heard was my call,

to the Holy One.

I was once tormented,

but now I am free;

there's been the fulfillment of my destiny.

Someday I will realize the *dream to write*

in the mean time I'll rest,

and then start to fight.

Let's forget our trouble and our tears

let's have some enjoyment through the years.

life has its hardships, yes indeed

but mirth and laughter can help

meet our needs.

When *will this pain be over?*

When will I find peace?

When will God take over

And give me sweet release?

Two peas in a pod

Two peas in a pod is what we were;

she was my entire life.

what a unique and special situation it was

we were held together by love and like.

she kept me from drowning,

she sewed on my wings,

the very surrounding

made our hearts sing.

Home sweet home is what she gave,

her love unconditional is what did save.

she knew how to love and genuinely care;

she knew how to cope and each burden to bear.

the discipline given seemed very severe,

but her heart was so good that it brought me a

tear.

how she could love and take me in;

the stars in the sky saw both of us win.

we were made for each other her daughter said;

we shared our heartaches and all of our dread.

but now she's at peace in God's heaven above,

we trembled o'er each other so great was our love.

Thoughts During Prayer

I knelt down in prayer

streaming down with tears.

there are lots of problems and many-a-care

that have passed by through the years.

And as I knelt down,

it seemed a sweet release.

There barely was a sound;

I felt a little peace.

The road may not be easy

our patience could run out.

on a day that's warm and breezy,

we could make our turnabout.

But as I put my feelings into words

I could then communicate

a touch of the absurd

and learn to tolerate.

Oh, in life the irony

is hard to comprehend.

we must balance with serenity

our thoughts until the end.

And even when things aren't what we plan,

it's just our destiny.

We do the very best we can,

and utter forth a plea.

Next time when I kneel down to pray,

next time when I will seek;

I'll try to find a brand-new way,

of learning to be meek.

Mercy comes to those who wait

from a God who is just and fair.

at times we often hesitate,

Our burden he will bear.

Anton and Mabel,

Anton and Mabel are very close neighbors.

Anton has done us many good favors.

Anton has been a long-time friend.

When he needs it, he gives us a hand.

He is a very good auto mechanic,

he has a "hello" which is a bright and dynamic.

Anton is also an excellent driver,

with him one can feel oneself safe as a rider.

Mabel how she loves to laugh,

whether you point a finger, or show a giraffe.

Mabel gave me a box of a musical present.

this was a gift which was useful and pleasant.

The gift was a way to surely acknowledge,

musical interest and musical knowledge.

No matter what their condition or mood,

Anton and Mabel love mother's good food.

we certainly talked over many a meal,

and did this with vigor, zest and with zeal.

But also this poem should not have been written

without mentioning their love for their teddy bear "Kitten."

Phyllis McDougall

I have a friend who is very dear;

the things which I tell her she is willing to hear.

while young she worked in a health food store,

this was her daily habit and chore.

through her work, many people she certainly did aid;

my own memories of her friendship,

Surely never will fade.

a person like Phyllis is so rare to meet,

she would much rather listen to music then eat.

she says in a voice which is soft and so sweet,

"Ich Liebe, Ich Liebe, Ich Liebe dicht."

(I love, I love, I love you)

Suffering and Torment

64, 8447 783337464 48 4273 86 2273

255 8447 7246

5433 6659 73367 86 23 863247

9484 5687 63 5677

288 6824 86 4246.

Suffering and torment

Oh, this suffering is hard to bear, all this torture, all this pain, life only seems to be unfair, with lots of loss, but much to gain

VELMA

VELMA, YOU ARE VERY SMART,

YOU UNDERSTAND THE HUMAN HEART.

SO MANY FRUITFUL CONVERSATIONS WE HAVE HAD,

AT TIMES I THINK THE LORD HAS LED,

OVER WHAT'S BEEN DONE AND WHAT'S BEEN SAID.

YOU MADE ME AWARE THAT BOOKS WERE MY FRIENDS,

THEY CAN BE A MEANS TO AN END.

VELMA, I'M GLAD I MET YOU;

YOU'VE LIVED MORE LIFE (THAN ME),

AND SEEN IT THROUGH.

My Precious Mama

What nicc mamas I have had,

they helped me realize, I' m not that bad.

auntie was very nice,

full of sweetness and lots of spice.

the most conscientious, wisest person I ever knew,

she was among the chosen few.

she was very wise;

I was like a beautiful child to her,

much to my surprise.

Belated birthday: 85

We began our afternoon journey,

to the home of a lady named Bernie.

the number of people there numbered nine,

we all left feeling very fine.

mother was made to feel like a queen

it made a very moving and touching scene.

mother was quiet and so very sweet

she was dressed very beautifully and neat.

she also took the time to listen,

how her eyes did sparkle and her face did

Glisten.

mother's spirit was joyful; serene

her face showed happiness

her spirit Did beam.

Bernie - how she loves to cultivate Flowers

she spends time in her garden by the hours and

hours.

she will do more than a greeting card send,

she's been to Erika, a very fine friend.

Bernie shown through with her personality

she showed us some gracious and fine hospitality.

the day went along like a day like that should,

we all left feeling so happy and good.

JOSEPHINE

JOSEPHINE, JOSEPHINE OF ALL PEOPLE YOU ARE KIND

YOU DID A VERY WONDERFUL WORK.

YOU GAVE INSIGHTS FOR MY MIND.

JOSIE, JOSEPHINE YOUR HEART IS FILLED WITH LOVE

YOU KNEW DR. HARRIS, WHO WAS HARMLESS AS A DOVE.

JOSIE, JOSIE YOU AREN't critical at ALL

YOU ARE JOSIE IN THE SUMMER, WINTER, SPRING AND IN THE FALL.

YOU OFTEN THINK OF OTHERS

EVEN THOUGH YOU HAD NO BROTHERS!

YOU HAD A SENSE OF HUMOR;

AND YOU TRY TO MEET A NEED,

ONE WAY IN WHICH YOU DID THIS

BY THE CARD WITH WHICH YOU FEED.

YOU'RE LIKE "BETH" IN "LITTLE WOMEN"

YOU TUCK ME IN JUST EVERY NIGHT.

IF YOU HAD KNOWN MY AUNTIE

YOU WOULD HAVE STOPPED OUR EVERY FIGHT.

(THAT THOUGHT GIVES ME SUCH DELIGHT)!

JOSIE GAVE ME A CARD:

MAY YOU FIND STRENGTH TO FACE TOMORROW

IN THE LOVE THAT SURROUNDS YOU TODAY.

Jim and Arlene

several times, we have seen

both Jim and his Arlene.

they are nice and warm and smart

and they act straight from the heart.

when they go up north for a drive,

they will often stop and arrive,

at our house for a while,

we visit well in style.

when it was his own turn,

Jim took the time to learn,

many poems and folks,

and serious thoughts and jokes.

no matter what life hands

Arlene always understands,

in her soft and gentle way,

both the dismal and the gay.

and also kind Arlene

is always nice and never mean.

we enjoy these friendly folks,

with Arlene's tact and Jim's smart jokes.

About Water

I have often had the notion

to walk over to the ocean

and just to be brave and admire a wave.

when I've looked at a pond

with thoughts that are fond

of getting your wish

while washing a fish.

I've had a big dream

when I've walked by a stream,

to walk through the woods

and to gather some goods.

quite often at tea

I have thought of the sea,

over there yonder

it's something to ponder.

very often I quiver

when I walk by the river,

and think of a snake

a-crossing the lake.

I've read in a book

of a babbling brook,

as a nice place to think, and

get water to drink.

Dogs

A dog is a man's best friend;

he'll be with you 'til the very end,

he's not only man's best friend, but woman's too,

a dog will always be loyal to you.

A composer wrote a piece called the dog's waltz;

this is true. and certainly not false!

whether one's a big or little cog

there should be no human who beats a dog.

sometimes even with our wrong dealings,

A dog forgives quickly if we've hurt his feelings.

A dogs image is of warmth and protection,

he accepts human beings and shows no objection.

among the dog's there's a distinguished feature;

he has a seventh sense; he's an intelligent creature.

dogs have worked to help out man

in whatever way they can,

the St. Bernard has saved people's lives,

scenting the trail; into the snow he dives.

a person can sometimes be the boss

but dogs have worked for the Red Cross.

A flower gardener may plant stocks

But, a dog can be a guardian of flocks.

a dog can sometimes be very kind,

serving as a companion to the blind.

a dog which is called a German Shepherd

resembles a dog; and not a leopard.

no matter where a dog it will roam,

his place is honored in the home.

yes, a dog is a human's best friend;

he'll be with his master 'til the very end.

Mysteries of life

There are birds that talk,

there are fish that walk,

yes, even a bird - can utter a word;

there are stars which fall

there is the Chinese wall,

there is the flower that blooms

there are musical tunes.

there are planets with moons,

there are many sand dunes.

the butterfly passes through various phases;

wise people turn into regular sages.

somebody invented the fiddle,

someone else will think of a riddle.

Life's a tremendous mystery

which only the grave will reveal.

all what is past is history,

what is present is that which is real,

it shapes how we think and we feel.

Ghosts of time

as one sees the days go by,

one thinks upon the ghosts of former times.

as one recalls it with a heavy sigh,

one hears afar the sound of a church bell chimes.

everything seems to gather in,

the ghost of days gone by,

and that of what has been,

will haunt us all until the day we die.

and there are moments when things seem to stand so still

that stars and trees preoccupy our mind.

And as one looks upon the semblance of the distance Hill

one awakens to the touch of the divine.

Nature

Oh, the wondrous stillness of God's green earth.

Oh, the wondrous warmth of a fire on the hearth.

Oh, the quiet of the birds in their migrating flight.

The soothing comfort of the night.

The sailors struggle while fighting the seas

the world at rest,

when there's no breeze.

The pot that's boiled on the stove,

the stately pride of trees within a grove.

A dream come true

Alas, buried beneath the deep white snow

where no stream or river doth flow

where no plant or flower doth grow

we get a chance to learn and to grow.

A dream from somewhere long ago

arises through the deep white snow,

and gives our lives a certain glow.

it suddenly becomes so real

we think and hope and deeply feel,

and pursue it with much zest and zeal,

and we wonder how this came about
when for a long time filled with doubt
one finally emerged upon this route
and reached one's destination
and without further hesitation
passed through every barrier and limitation.

one loses oneself in their endeavor

and knows the awakening will last forever,

one finds in life his cherished goal

peace for the mind,;

food for the soul.

The Holiday Jitters

We rush and hurry through the holidays

and forget to think and recall,

that there is truly a wonderful reason

for the meaning behind it all.

As we move in frustration through the shopping lines

worriedly buying presents and preparing dinners,

we know that we try to be on time,

during Christmas we know Christ was born for us sinners.

The holiday time is a little hard

but in childhood memories recall,

while to get all done and be on guard

we forget the meaning behind it all.

So take time out for the homebound and needy

we need time to reflect and recall;

with charity let us not be greedy,

let's remember the meaning behind it all.

Angels: Heavenly Hosts

High in the heavens an angel sings

and flies through the heavens on its gorgeous wings.

among the angel's missions and goals

is to minister to poor and suffering souls;

though we cannot see them with the eyes

they come to earth from their place on high.

angels come down to earth to minister

to all God's children against things that are sinister (evil).

we are always under their care

especially when we are not aware

of some lurking and unknown danger

(angels were with the Christ child

where he lay in the manger).

angels will guard and will always surround

this mission of theirs, they'll always abound

they will always protect us, and will always guard

especially when the going gets rough and the times get hard.

they are there, when there is a desperate need

they will always inspire us to do a kind deed.

they are present and always near,

when our hearts are trembling and filled with fear.

what shall we say of these hosts of light?

They are helping good to triumph o'er evil in the spiritual fight.

angels lift their heavenly gazes

and sing unto God their holy praises.

we can almost hear them sing allelujah

during the chorus of "Handel's hallelujah,"

or "The Vienna Boys Choir" with their angel-like voices

(and the Russian Orthodox girls singing around Easter)

to think about the hereafter and to make the right choices.

if we will only hold to our belief,

our angels will be present to help us in grief.

these wondrous messengers of goodwill,

will good and kindly thoughts instill,

and moments of truth our lives will fill.

angels are sent by God to bless

all of His children in times of distress;

in this constant battle over darkness and sin,

they will help us succeed in our struggle to win.

when we have been bad they are always sad

But when we have been good, they are Joyous and Glad.

They will inspire us and guide

how to change ourselves from inside.

if we only take the straight and narrow path,

they will help us escape, God's righteous wrath.

if we only decide the right to choose,

in this spiritual fight in the end we won't lose.

they're sent as messengers from God above,

to teach us how to live and to love.

it is no fable and no fairytale

that in their mission, they will not fail.

angels will help us to enter the fold,

and to heed to "the greatest story" that has ever been told.

Our angels are with us before and when

We are right with the Lord; (confess)

and; receive communion again.

www.ingramcontent.com/pod-product-compliance
Lightning Source LLC
Chambersburg PA
CBHW080535090426
42733CB00015B/2597